Look and See 1

ACTIVITY BOOK

Look and See ¹

ACTIVITY BOOK

1 TR: 0.1 Listen and point.

2 TR: 0.2 Sing and do.

STRUCTURE: *What's your name? My name's Jian.*

3 Draw and say.

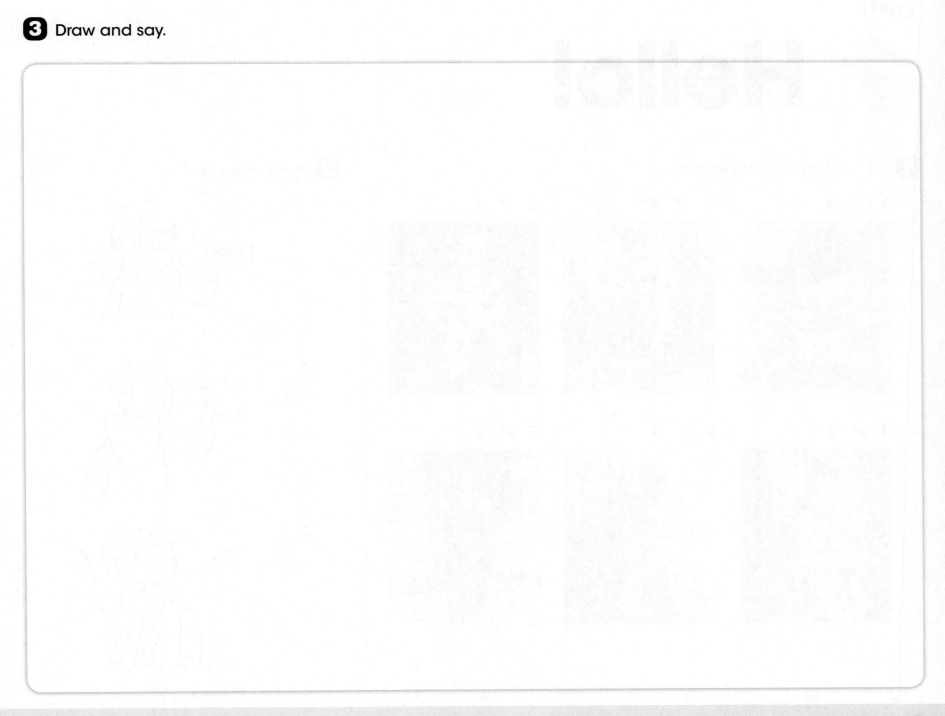

1 TR: 1.1 Listen. Circle ✔ or ✘.

1 (✔) ✘

2 ✔ ✘

3 ✔ ✘

4 ✔ ✘

5 ✔ ✘

6 ✔ ✘

2 Point and say.

1

2

3

NEW WORDS: *Hello! Goodbye. Say hello. Wave goodbye. Stand up. Sit down. Open your book. Close your book.*

1 TR: 1.2 Listen and circle.

1

2

3

STRUCTURE: *How are you? I'm fine, thank you.*

7

1 TR: 1.3 Sing and point.

2 Look and circle.

VALUE Make friends.

1

2

SONG AND VALUE: *Make friends.*

1 Trace.

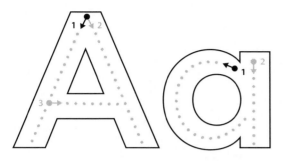

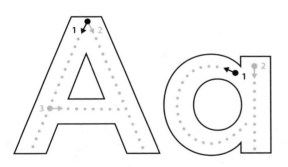

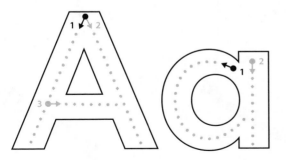

2 Draw yourself.

1 TR: 2.1 Listen and circle.

1

2

3

4

5

6

1 TR: 2.2 Listen. Circle ✔ or ✘.

1 ✔ ✘ **2** ✔ ✘ **3** ✔ ✘ **4** ✔ ✘ **5** ✔ ✘

2 Color. Ask and answer.

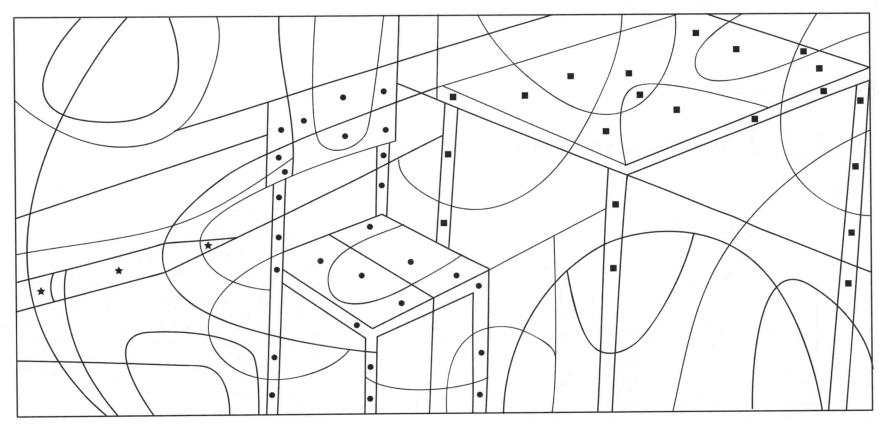

1 TR: 2.3 Color. Sing and point.

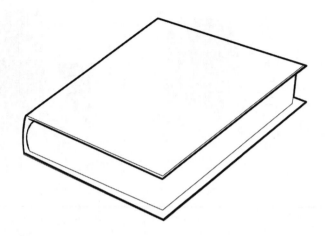

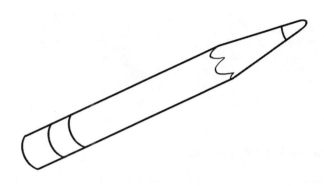

2 Look and circle.

VALUE Take care of your things.

1

2

1 Trace.

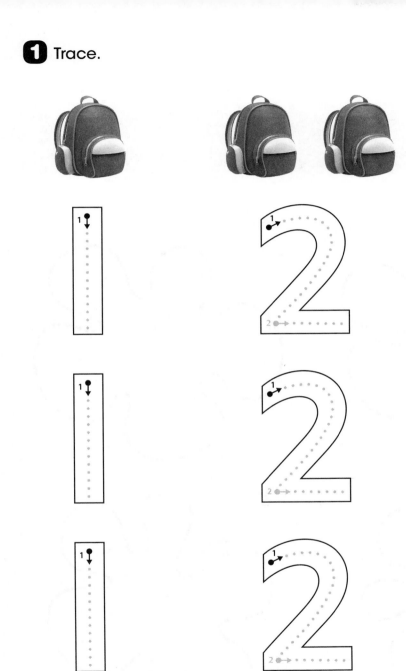

2 Draw your school.

3 Colors

1 TR: 3.1 Listen and color.

NEW WORDS: *blue, green, orange, paint, purple, red, yellow*

1 TR: 3.2 Listen and color. Then ask and answer.

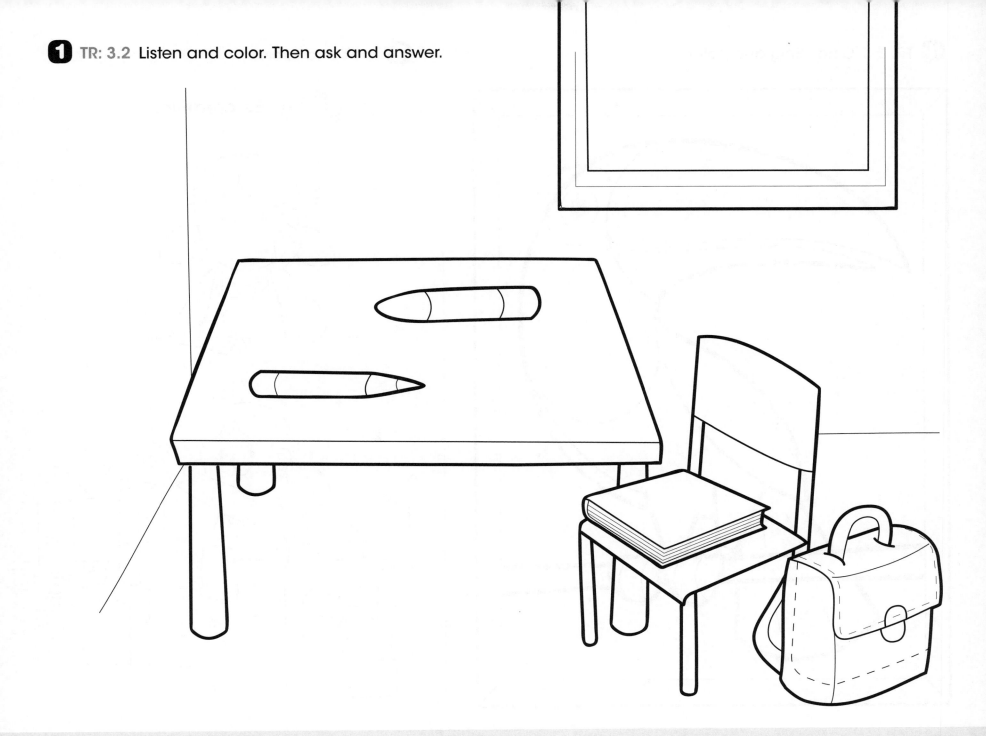

STRUCTURE: *What color is the book? It's red.*

1 TR: 3.3 Color. Sing and point.

2 Look and circle.

VALUE Be creative.

1

2

1 Trace.

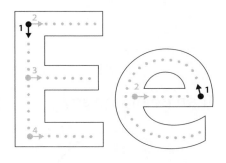

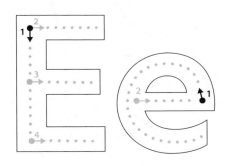

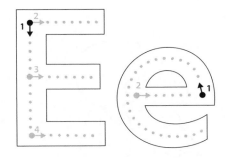

2 TR: 3.4 Listen and color.

1

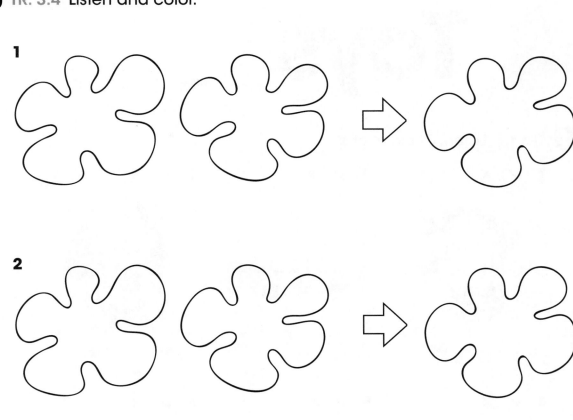

2

3

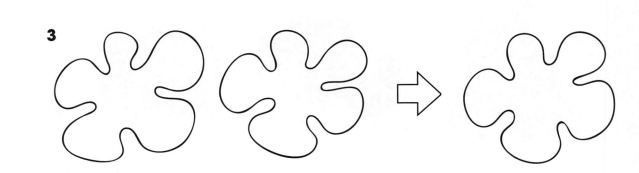

UNIT 4 Toys

1 TR: 4.1 Listen. Circle ✔ or ✗.

1 (✔) ✗

2 ✔ ✗

3 ✔ ✗

4 ✔ ✗

5 ✔ ✗

6 ✔ ✗

2 Color. Then point and say.

1

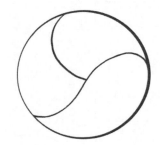

2

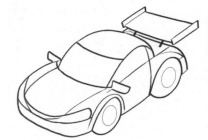

3

18 **NEW WORDS:** *ball, bus, car, doll, puppet, teddy bear, train*

1 TR: 4.2 Listen and circle.

1

  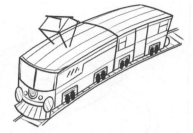

2

1 TR: 4.3 Listen, point, and count. Then color.

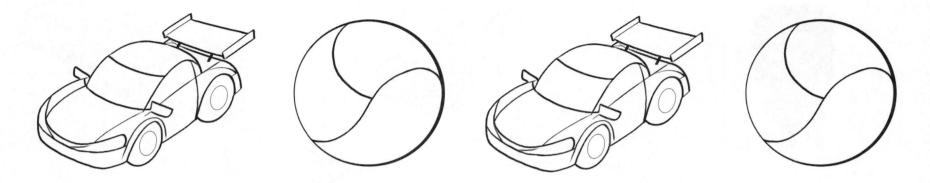

2 Look and circle.

VALUE Share your toys.

1

2

1 Trace.

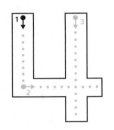

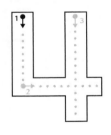

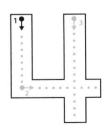

2 Draw your favorite toy.

5 Let's Move!

1 TR: 5.1 Listen and point.

2 Trace and say. Then color.

NEW WORDS: *arms, body, feet, hands, head, legs, tummy*

 Heads: Move 1    Tails: Move 2

START

   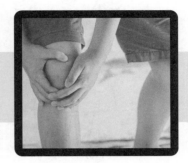

 Move Back

 1  FINISH

STRUCTURE: *Touch your head. Move your hands.*

1 TR: 5.2 Listen and color. Then sing.

2 Look and circle.

VALUE Be active.

1

2

1 Trace.

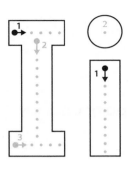

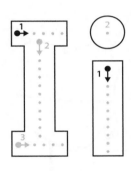

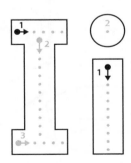

1

2

3

1 TR: 6.1 Listen and circle.

1

2

3

4

5

6

2 Color. Then point and say.

NEW WORDS: *apple, banana, carrot, cracker, milk, orange, water*

1 TR: 6.2 Listen and circle.

1

2

1 TR: **6.3** Listen and color. Then sing and point.

2 Look and circle.

VALUE Choose healthy food.

1

2

1 Trace.

2 Draw your favorite tree.

UNIT 7 My Family

1 TR: 7.1 Listen and match.

1

2

3

A

B

C

2 Point and say.

NEW WORDS: *brother, dad, grandma, grandpa, mom, photo, sister*

1 Draw your family and say. Then color.

1 TR: 7.2 Listen and match. Then sing.

2 Look and circle.

Be good to your family.

1

2

3

1 Trace.

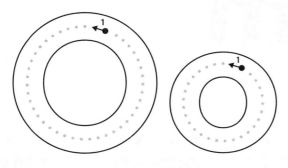

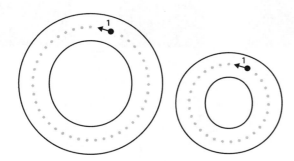

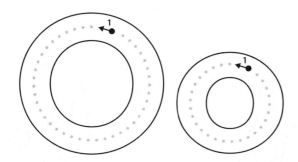

2 TR: 7.3 Listen and match.

1   2

8 On the Farm

1 TR: 8.1 Listen. Circle ✔ or ✗.

1 ✔ ✗
2 ✔ ✗
3 ✔ ✗
4 ✔ ✗
5 ✔ ✗
6 ✔ ✗
7 ✔ ✗

2 Match and say.

1
2
3
4

A
B
C
D

NEW WORDS: *cat, chicken, cow, dog, goat, horse, sheep*

1 TR: 8.2 Listen. Circle ✔ or ✗.

1 ✔ ✗

2 ✔ ✗

3 ✔ ✗

4 ✔ ✗

5 ✔ ✗

2 Ask and answer.

1
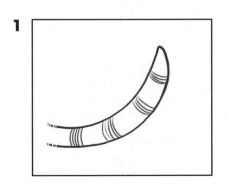

2
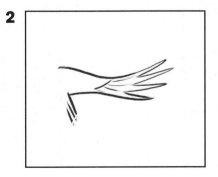

3

4

STRUCTURE: *Is it a cow? No, it isn't. Is it a horse? Yes, it is.*

1 TR: 8.3 Sing and point.

2 Look and circle.

VALUE   Take care of animals.

1

2

3

① Trace.

② Match and say.

1

A

2

B

3

C

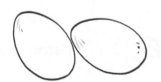

My Clothes

1 TR: 9.1 Listen and match.

1 2 3 4 5 6

2 TR: 9.2 Listen and color.

1   2   3   4   5   6

NEW WORDS: *hat, jacket, shoes, shorts, socks, T-shirt; black, brown, white*

1 TR: 9.3 Listen and color. Then match and say.

STRUCTURE: *My T-shirt is orange. My shorts are red.*

39

1 TR: 9.4 Listen and color. Then sing.

2 Look and circle.

VALUE Dress yourself.

1

2

3

1 Trace.

2 Trace, match, and say.

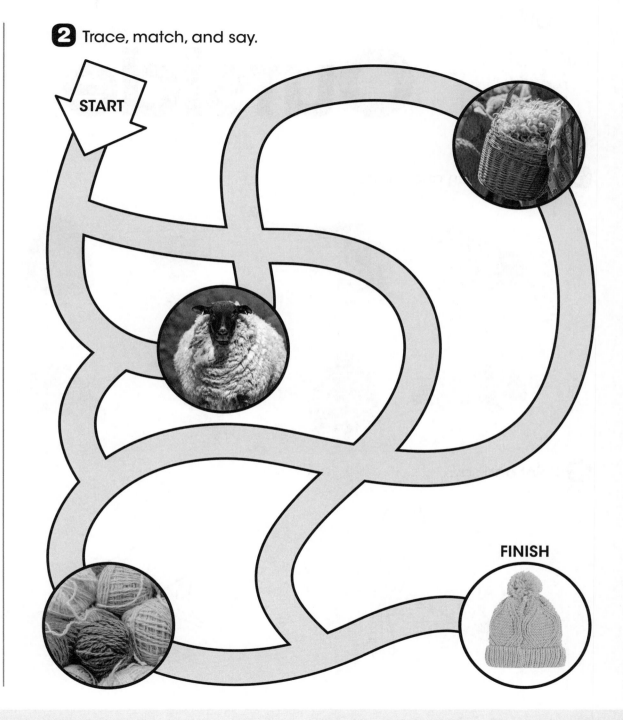

START

FINISH

10 Outside

1 TR: 10.1 Listen and circle.

1

2

3

4

5

6

2 Point and say.

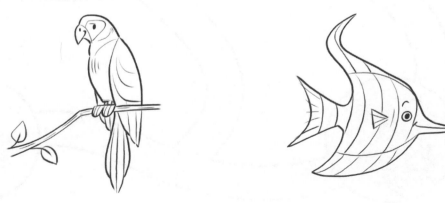

NEW WORDS: *bird, fish, flower, frog, leaf, rainbow, tree*

1 TR: 10.2 Listen and circle. Then find.

1 2 3

1 2 3

1 2 3

4 5 6

4 5 6

6 7 8

6 7 8

1 TR: 10.3 Listen and circle. Then sing.

1 2 3

3 4 5

2 Look and circle.

Explore outside.

1

2

3

1 Trace.

2 TR: 10.4 Listen and color.

1

2

3

BERLITZ MID-LEVEL TEST

Please do not open

Writing score: _____ / 50   *Speaking score: _____ / 50*

Name: _____

Listen and circle. (6 points)

Example:

1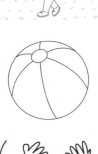

2

3

Color. (8 points)

4    **5**    **6**    **7**

red   **blue**   **green**   **yellow**

Listen. Circle ✔ or ✘. **(8 points)**

Example:

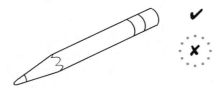
✔

∴✘∴

  ✔
✘

9 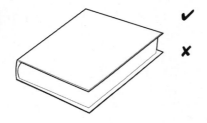 ✔
✘

10 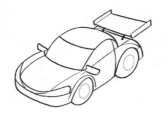 ✔
✘

11  ✔
✘

Trace and write. **(18 points)**

12 A A   a a

13 E E

14 I I

Count and write. (6 points)

Example:

3

15

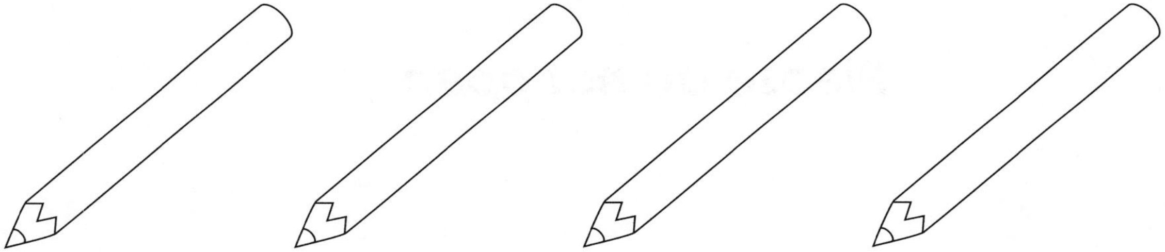

16

17

18 Write your first name. (4 points)

BERLITZ END-OF-LEVEL TEST

Please do not open

Writing score: _____/50   *Speaking score: _____/50*

Name: _____

Listen and circle. **(6 points)**

Example:

2

3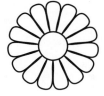

Color. **(8 points)**

4  **5** **6** **7**

black   **brown**   **white**   **orange**

Listen. Circle ✔ or ✗. (8 points)

Example:

   ✔
                       ✗

8    ✔   ✗

9    ✔   ✗

10    ✔   ✗

11    ✔   ✗

Circle the same letter. (18 points)

Example:

U   u   o   a   o   u   u

12 i   T   I   L   T   I   I

13 A   a   o   u   a   o   a

14 e   F   T   E   E   F   E

Count and write. (10 points)

Example:

9

15

16

17

18

19

Unit 3 Color and say.

Color and say.

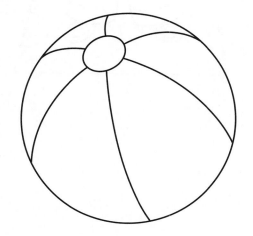

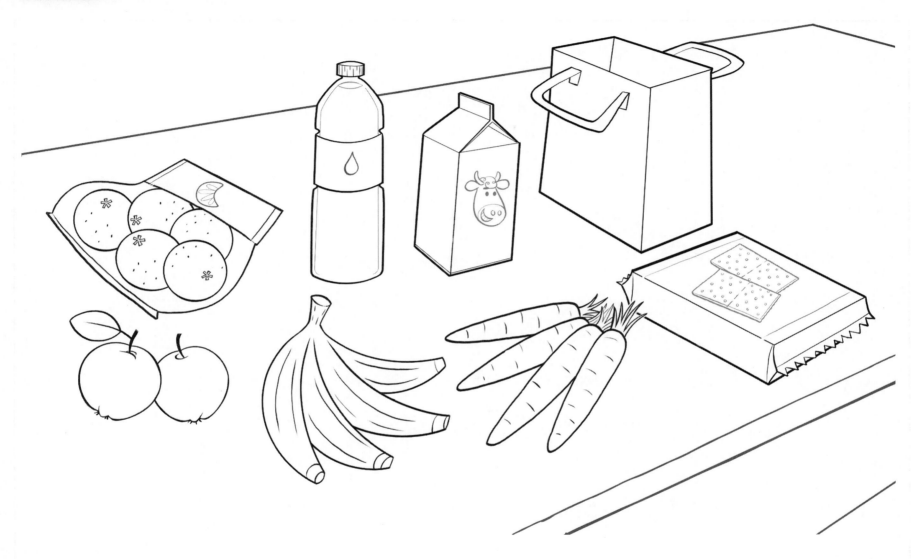

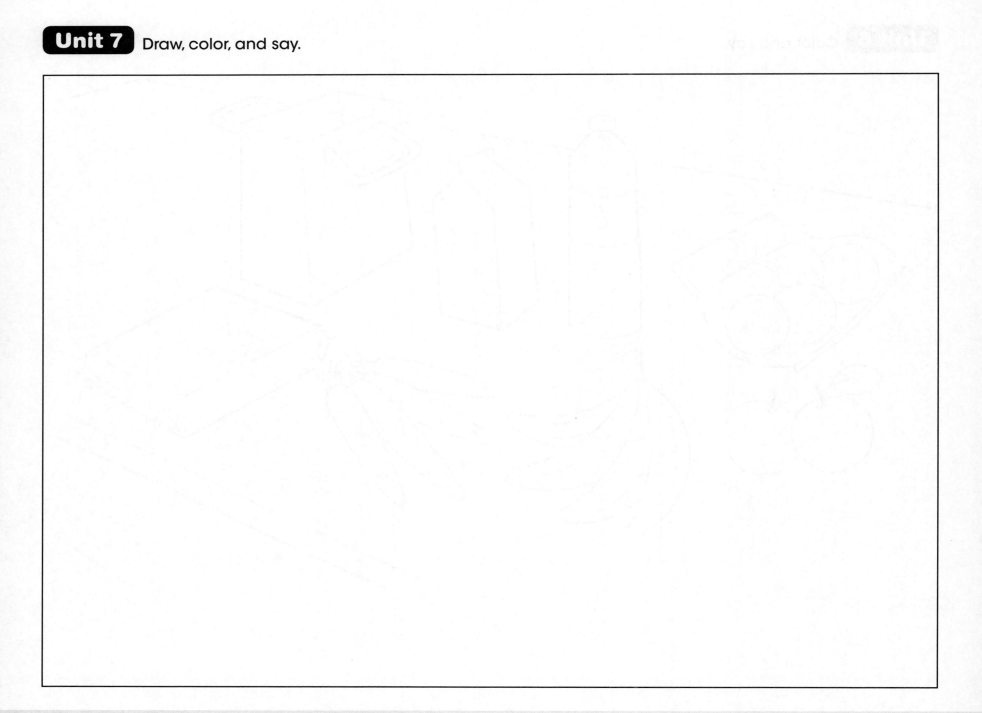

CREDITS